A REMARKABLE PRACTICE

Developing Leaders Personally & Professionally

BEN FINCH

A Remarkable Practice
Developing Leaders Personally & Professionally
by Ben Finch

Printed in the United States of America

ISBN 978-1-60647-968-1

For more information or to order group copies of this book, visit: www.thevisiblegroup.net. As well, you will find information on how The Visible Group can be strategic in meeting your organization's marketing & design needs.

If you would like to schedule a leadership workshop or consult, please visit www.laconsults.com or email: ben@laconsults.com

www.xulonpress.com

"With upright heart he tended them,
& guided them with a skillful hand."

Psalm 78:72

"Never doubt it—there will be leadership,
good or bad."

Gaines Dobbins, Professor & Author

"Leadership is an action, not a word."

Richard P. Cooley, American Banker

CONTENTS

To My Family,
My wife Joy & our son, Brennan.
You are the ones I want to lead the most!
I love you.

LETTER FROM THE AUTHOR

As best I can remember I have always been this way; I guess you might say that I am driven to better myself. My friends and family think I am discontent unless I am doing something challenging. I suppose they are correct. I prefer to think of myself as a maximizer, trying to take profit of every day. I have this yearning inside of me to take full advantage of my God-given talents. This yearning often manifests itself in me striving to meet another goal such as: an additional course of study, a new product for my company, certification in another area, an additional job venture, learning a new language, or even recording a album with my band. I love the sense of accomplishment that comes when you stretch yourself beyond what you thought imaginable.

This book is written for you who desire to be a better leader. Maybe you want to achieve something great in your work, church, or even family. Possibly, you have tried many things but need practical insight into how to make it happen. Or, maybe you have steered off course and need reminded of what is important. I hope you take this process seriously and approach it with great passion. But be cautious, in order to lead others; we must first learn to lead ourselves. And that is possibly the greatest challenge. It is my hope that you approach leadership with integrity. Renowned author Lewis Smedes stated, "Integrity is a bigger thing than telling the truth. It is about being a certain kind of person. It is about being people who know who we are and what we are, and it is about being true to what we are even when it could cost us more than we should like to pay."

A Remarkable Practice is a collection of leadership principles I have gathered and put into practice in the organizations I have served. They are not merely ideas but are a way of life for me. I hope you would see this reflected in my actions.

Esse Quam Videri! "To be rather than appear!"

Ben Finch

August 7, 2008

Why do you need to grow as a leader?

1. What got you here will not sustain you.

2. An organization cannot out grow its people.

3. Leaders must grow their people in order to grow the organization.

4. People cannot grow unless the leader grows.

5. The competition "will" out grow you.

6. Leadership determines the level of one's effectiveness.

Developing the Leader Within You, John C. Maxwell

INTRODUCTION

W hat makes a practice remarkable? I suppose there are
many aspects to this question. I must first clarify that
I am using the work, "practice," both as a noun meaning
an organization as well as a verb, describing an action or
behavior. The aspects that make a practice remarkable are
many. Referring to an organization, you could focus on sales
and productivity, low turnover rate and job satisfaction,
customer service and hospitality, technology and marketing,
etc. If these aspects exceed the competition, you may be
tempted to consider that organization remarkable. Yet, this
can be misleading. You may also want to consider if the
company operates with integrity or determine what kind of
impact the organization has upon others. This too matters.
Or, what about the quality of leaders the company produces?
Are they making a positive difference in their communities?
Yes, this too should be assessed.

With these critical questions in mind, I invite you to *A
Remarkable Practice*. This leadership development guide
will walk you through a number of characteristics that I deem
vital for both a healthy organization and for an exceptional
leader. They are not complete. In order to fully understand the
complexity of leadership within an organization, my research
would never cease. Extensive writings have been consulting
in producing this book, yet researchers and authors must

admit that organizations are constantly changing, therefore continual study is required. What I hope to accomplish in this work is to organize and teach in a simple, practical manner certain attributes that make organizations and leaders stand out among their peers.

I am choosing to focus on 5 things that make a practice remarkable; this is dealt with in Chapters 1-5. As well, I am using terms found in music to describe these aspects: musicians, melody, harmony, rhythm, and audience. I realize readers have a broad range of interest, yet it seems we all enjoy music. Although we have different preferences, all can agree that music is the universal language. Plus, I hope the leadership principles discussed in this book are easier to remember when you can relate them to something with which you are familiar. Chapter 1: Musicians, deals with the dynamics of a healthy team. Chapter 2: Melody is a look at the fundamental purpose of an organization. Chapter 3: Harmony, evaluates communication within a company and how it reinforces the organization's purposes. Chapter 4: Rhythm is an overview of human systems that provide consistency for the company. Chapter 5: Audience discusses the role customer service plays in making one organization stand above the rest.

Chapter 6: Leadership Action Plan is quite different than the previous chapters. In this chapter, I provide an action plan at strengthening one's personal leadership ability. Then, I examine the six key relationships for leadership development and offer practical suggestions on how to improve these relationships.

Following each chapter will be a notes section you may use to make notes about ideas that stood out within the chapter. If you realize you need to improve in your leadership in certain areas, make note of it. Then, jot down a few ideas you have about taking action for change.

remarkable: (adj.)

worthy of attention, striking

CHAPTER 1

MUSICIANS: *Team*

"When spider webs unite, they can tie up a lion."
Egyptian Proverb

"Michael, if you can't pass it, you can't play."
Dean Smith, to Michael Jordan

Most of us have been a part of a team at some point in our lives. For many of us it was when we competed in team sports. Others may have been on a debate team or drama team. Or, your employer may have you structured to work in teams. You may consider you family as your team, and I hope that you do. Regardless of what kind of team, there is a constant fiber of truth that is thread in every team: *the success of every team is dependent upon the contribution of each team member.*

For the past few years I have played in a band. When I was in college I began playing the guitar and I made my living as a musician for many years afterward. There is something magic that happens when you have been playing with a group of musicians for an extended season and things seem to click; we like to say that we are in the "cut."

What I love about the band I play with now is that these guys are true professionals. What I mean is that they are not only extremely proficient in their instruments, but they are teachable. We have learned that sometimes what is best for a certain song isn't the same in other songs. There are songs we perform that the electric guitar doesn't play until halfway through the song. Other times, we all stop playing except the drummer, who keeps the rhythm going. Some of my favorite songs begin softly but climax during the bridge. What I love about this is that we all know our role. Although my drummer wishes he could play the bass, he wouldn't dare try it in a concert. Why? Because it is not his role. He brings to the group what he is proficient in and we all benefit from his talent.

Some of these things you may have never thought about until now. You may not hear how many different instruments play on a certain song on the radio. It would probably surprise you if you knew. Plus, it may not occur to you that every instrument doesn't play during the entire song. If they did, you might not appreciate the emotion the song seems to capture.

Imagine the chaos that would occur if we attempted to play instruments in which we were not trained. Or, you could cringe at the thought of every person playing in a different musical key. It would be a disaster.

Key Point: We all bring different talents to our teams, yet the success of the team is determined by our ability to trust and collaborate with one another.

I know this sounds elemental, but trust me, it is a rare sight. Few too many of us are willing to set our egos aside for the good of the team. It seems we would rather accept only plans that we can do by ourselves; what a pity. As Mark Twain stated, "It is amazing what can be done if no one cares who gets the credit." I couldn't agree more.

To further reinforce this point, I would like to share with you 5 Barriers to a Remarkable Team. They are an adaptation from author & business consultant Patrick Lencioni's *5 Dysfunctions of a Team* (as a side note, read everything he has written- excellent!).

Barriers to a Remarkable Team

1. Distrust among Team Members
2. Fear of Confrontation
3. Apathy
4. Lack of Accountability
5. Focus on Achievement of Individual Results

Let's take a moment to discuss the 5 barriers.

Distrust among Team Members

Lack of trust among team members seems to be a root of all sorts of problems. Simply consider the outcome of a marriage when two partners do not trust one another. When team members cannot trust one another and do not believe that their colleagues' intentions are good, productiveness is highly limited. Rarely, if ever, can the goal of a team be accomplished when members are unwilling to be vulnerable to their mates. Trust prerequisites a certain amount of vulnerability to others.

Fear of Confrontation

It seems that our present culture places way too much value upon tolerance. So much that even as leaders we are unwilling to confront behaviors that are detrimental to our organizations. I admit that confrontation is difficult, but it is pertinent to team health. As leaders, we must realize that this is part of our responsibility and accept our role. For far too long have we been unwilling to "speak the truth in love."

23

We must remember that sometimes the most loving thing we can do is to confront wrong behavior in an effort to help others grow.

Business consultant Rick Packer states, "we need people around us who will tell us what we need to hear as opposed to people who tell us what we want to hear."

Apathy

From my experience, apathy sets in when people do not believe that their contribution is being valued. In these kind of environments, employees begin to view their work as merely a paycheck rather than an investment in a career. Great teams allow ideas to be shared openly and are valued equally, yet nobody is offended when their idea is not implemented. When teams operate with such openness, buy-in from every team member follows.

Lack of Accountability

Accountability is simply holding team members to the agreed upon standards. This includes a willingness among team members to call one another out on behaviors that are not up to par. Rather than simply avoid one another or to gossip behind each other's backs, great teams know that they are going to be held to the set standards. Often out of a desire to not let teammates down, people will correct their behavior.

Focus on Achievement of Individual Results

When members begin to place higher value upon individual results rather than collective, issues are soon to follow. No great team can allow this behavior for an extended period of time. If organizations are going to be successful, it will take the collective results of each team member, regardless of their roles. As Coach Fuller, my college soccer coach, used to say, "Gentlemen, we win as a team and we lose as a team. Whether you played the game of your life does not matter if we did not win."

Take a moment to reflect on your "team." Do you feel like you are part of a remarkable team? Or, do you identify with the barriers that may be keeping your team from being a cohesive unit?

If you were to name the top 2 barriers of your team, what would they be? Why?

•

•

In what ways do *you* hinder the team's progression? How might you personally improve in one of these 5 key areas? Record your thoughts:

•

•

•

Now, let us focus our attention on the characteristics that aid in team health.

Characteristics of a Remarkable Team

1. Trust one Another
2. Respectful Confrontation
3. Commitment to Team
4. High Accountability
5. Focus on Achievement of Collective Results

Trust one Another

Consider some ways that you can build trust among your team members:

- *Example:* Initiate conversations that are centered on another's values and interests.

-

-

-

Respectful Confrontation

Are you a leader who has developed a pattern of avoiding confrontation? If you are like me, this is not your favorite aspect of leadership. Yet, it seems great teams do not avoid conflict. Rather than avoid this necessary aspect of teamwork, why not create an environment where team members feel the freedom to conflict over ideas, yet still value one another.

Playing sports at a collegiate level taught me greatly about confrontation and conflict. There were a few teammates of mine that seemed to disagree about everything when we were "off the field." Yet, it amazed me at the loyalty they would have toward one another and our team. I suppose what made the dynamic so unique was the environment of trust our coach was careful to maintain.

Commitment to Team

One's lack of commitment is often the result of feeling undervalued by other team members. When people do not sense that their contribution is esteemed, their buy-in is minimal. What can you do as a leader to initiate team members to take greater ownership in the team, thus resulting in greater commitment? Brainstorm some ideas:

- *Example:* Have team members develop a business model of where they see the greatest potential for growth in the next 5 years.

-

-

-

High Accountability

Are your team members willing to hold each other accountable? If not, why do you think they are unwilling?

What can you do to help raise the standards of accountability within your organization?

Focus on Achievement of Collective Results

Many organizations seem to reward employees based solely upon achievement of individual results. It is no wonder there is no spirit of unity. When recognition is only achieved through individual performance, people begin to look out for only themselves. I am careful to suggest systems that are based upon the achievement of collective results. The president of our consulting firm, Tammy Leonard, has developed a shared earnings program that is based upon the achievement of all team members. It has made an amazing impact upon team motivation.

During graduate school I was a part-time manager for a retail-clothing store. I began to have some fairly major issues among staff members that I quickly realized were based upon too great of focus on individual results. Our team members were receiving 'spiffs' based upon their sales performance.

This led to employees ringing up other peoples' sales under their numbers and fighting over customers; it was ugly. And, I was not empowered to make the necessary changes for team health.

Take a moment to consider your organization. Do the systems you have in place reinforce the value of collective team results or individual achievement? What can you do in order to turn the focus upon the achievement of collective results? Jot down some notes below:

•

•

•

It is highly important to diagnose whether or not your team is healthy. Sometimes, this can only be accomplished from an outsider's perspective. I once heard it said that many don't know they are ill because they have never witnessed health. The following is a model by consultant Patrick Lencioni, (www.thetablegroup.com) titled *Smart + Healthy*. It may serve as a guide to help you diagnose your organization's health.

I would dare say that most teams within organizations that I have the privilege to consult are *smart*. They employ methods such as strategy, technology, financial plans, partnerships, and marketing. Yet, it is rare that I see a *smart + healthy* team. *Healthy* teams have relatively no office politics and minimal confusion about responsibilities, duties, and communication. These teams typically have low staff turnover as well. Who wouldn't want to work in this environment? Last, there is high productivity and high morale among team members.

The "Typical" Team *Smart*	The "Healthy" Team *Smart + Healthy*
Smart teams possess these characteristics and employ these methods for business success.	*Smart + Healthy* teams possess all the characteristics of a *Smart* team with the addition of the following:
1. Strategy	1. Minimal Politics
2. Technology	2. Minimal Confusion
3. Financial Plans	3. Low Turnover
4. Partnerships	4. High Productivity
5. Marketing	5. High Morale
	Patrick Lencioni, The Table Group

Based upon the model above, what areas within your organization would you consider unhealthy? Are you experiencing high turnover, low morale, etc.? Identify them here:

-

-

-

Name some examples within organizations you have worked for that you would diagnose as being unhealthy.

-

-

Have you considered the difference between business success and business health? What steps can you take to become healthy again?

-

-

NOTES:

CHAPTER 2

MELODY: *Purpose*

"A ship at harbor is safe,
but that's not what it's built for."
Coffee, from the band G.R.I.T.S.

"The secret to success is constancy of purpose."
*Benjamin Disraeli, 1804-1881, British Statesman,
Prime Minister*

Have you ever had a song stuck in your head that you heard on the radio? Sometimes you do not even realize it until hours later when you cannot quit humming the chorus. This happens to me on occasions.

I am not necessarily partial to any genre of music. I find myself listening to anything from alternative rock to blues, classical to jazz, gospel hymns to country, and yes, hip-hop on occasions. I cannot help it; I like all kinds of music. I'm particularly drawn to songs that have a nice melody. The melody is a sequence of single notes tied together. In general, it is what most people remember about a song; if you were to ask someone how a song goes, they will probably hum you the melody. I'm no music major, but it seems to be the foundation of the song.

Think about it, you can have a very simple song that is sung accapella by one person, no instruments. Yet, the melody remains.

Now, let's think about your situation. If you were to come up with one reason why your organization exists, what would it be? Try to be very simple and direct; one sentence should be plenty. Make sure you write this down.

My organization exists to:

This is your purpose statement. It is the melody, if you will, of your organization. Like music, when you remove the other musicians, singers, crowd, & etc., this is what remains. It is your organization in its simplest form and the reason it exists.

This purpose statement should not be very complicated. If it is, you will need to simplify. Truth is, if it is difficult for you to remember or recite, then it is too complex and people within your organization will not internalize it. If you do not personally embody the values of your purpose statement, it will not exist in the values of your employees.

For example, consider the purpose statement of a marketing and design firm that I founded, The Visible Group. We exist to: *Be creative in our approach, to inspire our customer, and improve their image!*

Sounds a little too basic doesn't it? I'm not even sure if it would fly in business school, but everything we do as a company is intentional. Every product we design and every moment we capture is intended to *create, inspire, and improve*. I do not ask our designers and developers to recite this, but I do ask them to have these intentions. These three ideas guide our every decision; they guide *my* every decision for the company. Within the realm of marketing and design, I am able to be creative in my approach, to inspire my customer, and to improve their current image. If I cannot accomplish this, I need to let someone else do it.

Patrick Lencioni helps organizations achieve clarity in purpose. He offers a series of basic questions that you should ask to help guide your organization's purpose:

1. Why does the organization exist, and what difference does it make in the world?

2. What behavioral values are irreplaceable and fundamental?

3. What business are we in, and against whom do we compete?

4. How does our approach differ from that of our competition?

5. What are our goals this month, this quarter, this year, next year, five years from now?

6. Who has to do what for us to achieve our goals this month, this quarter, this year, next year, five years from now?

Patrick Lencioni
The Four Obsessions of An Extraordinary Executive

Key Point: Your organization's purpose must be the driving force of everything your company does and it must exist in the values of your employees.

May I further challenge you with something I was taught a few years ago. I have a great friend who is a recording artist, his name is Nathan Wesley Smith. Truth is told, he has probably taught me a majority of what I know musically. One day we were playing guitar together and in the midst of a conversation he told me, "Ben, less is more." This simple statement has proved formative in my life. It has been a filter through which I make decisions in various arenas of life: business, church, family, leadership, and music. His intention was to help me understand that when communicating through music that the message needs to be simple, to "cut out the fluff."

Many people need this message, especially in organizations. A great question to ask: Is there anything that we are doing that is outside of our foundational purpose? If so, I would challenge you to cut it out. Do only what furthers your purpose. As Dr. Howard Hendricks said, "The secret of concentration is elimination." Leaders must line every activity up against the purpose of the organization.

Consider the following illustration:

I recently read an article about a drill bit manufacturer who hired a new CEO. After hearing presentations by top managers from across the company about division performance, the CEO gathered them together and explained: "There is no market for drill bits. The only market is for holes and as soon as somebody invents a better way to create a hole, we're out of business."

Needless to say, this CEO brought a new perspective to his organization. David Rockefeller, prominent American banker, would agree, "The #1 function of the top executive is to establish the purpose of the organization."

Questions for Reflection

1. Is your organization's purpose driving its every activity?

2. Are there areas/activities in your organization that need to be reevaluated because they are distracting from your core purpose? What are they?

3. Consider the "drill bit" illustration. What market is your company in? What new methods would you consider to help achieve your purpose?

4. Is the vision for the organization being communicated on a regular basis through various mediums? If not, why? How will you change this?

NOTES:

CHAPTER 3

HARMONY: *Communication*

"Communication is the real work of leadership."
Nitin Nohria, Harvard Business School

"The single biggest problem in communication is
the illusion that it has taken place."
George Bernard Shaw, Irish Playwright

Harmony complements the melody. If you will continue with the music analogy, you will recognize that as harmony adds different pitches to the melody, creating a pleasing sound, so does proper communication to an organization's purpose. Let me explain.

Harmony never overtakes the melody; it serves the melody.

Good communication in an organization occurs when her people clearly understand the goals and values that exist within the company. It is not merely a slogan on the company logo, it is in the DNA of every project. Employees know and hear this message constantly and they see it in one another's actions. Nobody is kept in the dark and personal agendas are set aside.

Let us evaluate what good communication looks like and consider our personal preferences when it comes to communication. Answer the following:

If you were to name someone who you believe to be an excellent communicator, who would that be?

Write their name here:

What makes this person an excellent communicator? Try to name some of their attributes that make them good at communicating, be very specific.

- *Example:* They are able to communicate on a level that everyone can grasp.

-

-

-

-

An ancient Hebrew proverb states, "The teacher has not taught unless the student has learned." This communication principle is fundamental for having a *Remarkable Practice*. Simply put, great leaders are good communicators. And all good communicators know that they have not successfully communicated unless the recipient receives the message. Upon receiving the message, the recipient acts. Business consultant and lecturer, Fred Smith, stated, "We communicate only when people listen. And unless people follow us, we're not leaders."

You must realize that your organization's purpose is reinforced by effective communication.

Years ago I discovered an outline for communication that literally changed my life. I teach these principles every chance I get, whether to doctors and staff, husbands and wives, pastors and teachers, etc. It is a wonderful tool to enhance one's communication abilities. I reference them prior to my every public speaking engagement.

5 Important Questions You Must Be Able to Answer Before Communicating with Excellence

1. What do they (*my intended audience*) need to know?

2. Why do they need to know it?

3. What do they need to do?

4. Why do they need to do it?

5. How can I help them remember?

This is a great communication outline to follow in any setting, whether public or private. Although the author's intent is for teaching, I find it beneficial for the transfer of any information.

Key Point: Great communicators know that they have not successfully communicated unless the recipient receives the message. And upon reception, the recipient acts.

Communication occurs on many levels and through various mediums within an organization. Countless communicate through email & text messaging, others transfer ideas at the water-cooler, while some engage in a lunch meeting, etc.

I am not telling you what mediums to use, but simply providing outlines for how good communication occurs.

May I offer you the opportunity to consider your ability to communicate:

On a scale of 1 to 10. 1 being poor, 10 being excellent. How would you rate your ability to communicate?

1   2   3   4   5   6   7   8   9   10

How do you think those who work with you would rate you?

1   2   3   4   5   6   7   8   9   10

What about your family?

1   2   3   4   5   6   7   8   9   10

How would you rate your listening skills?

1   2   3   4   5   6   7   8   9   10

When others are speaking with you, do they have your full attention? How do you think others would rate your listening skills?

1   2   3   4   5   6   7   8   9   10

Answer the following questions very carefully with all honesty. Record your answers:

1. Do you communicate clearly? In other words, have you carefully thought through what you are wanting to say before you say it? Why or why not?

2. Do you embody the attributes that you find necessary for excellent communication?

3. How might you improve as a communicator?

4. How can you use technology to enhance or simplify communication within your organization?

5. Based upon the *5 Important Questions*, how can these tools help you to become a more effective communicator?

Excellent communication is rare. When it boils down to it, it is probably at the heart of most organizational problems. *T & D Magazine*, a Ken Blanchard company, ranked "Interpersonal Communication Skills" as the 2nd most difficult challenge for employee development (June 2006). If you dare sit in on an average staff meeting, you may be surprised at how little is actually accomplished. At best, many employees are simply trying to "make it through" the meeting.

But it doesn't have to be this way. One organization I worked for had the healthiest staff meetings I've ever seen. The dialogue was quick, decisions were made, and everyone was involved. Although the "boss" or department head made the final decision, everyone was heard. I must confess though, it got rowdy at times and conflict frequently occurred over certain ideas. Yet, when a decision was made, we gave our support and backed it as if it were our own. Feelings weren't hurt over comments made or ideas shot down; we trusted one another.

I have outlined a few communication practices to keep in mind:

1. Be Simple

People are swamped with information. As leaders we must learn how to send uncomplicated key messages to one another.

"The ability to simplify means to eliminate the unnecessary so that the necessary may speak."
Hans Hoffmann,
German-born American
abstract expressionist

"You need a talent for simplicity—for saying things in a few words. GE's Jack Welch is a good example. He is astonishingly articulate and able to convey complicated concepts in just a few phrases."
Joe Badaracco,
Harvard Business School

2. Be Repetitive, Be Repetitive, Be Repetitive

Employees need to hear the same message numerous times in numerous ways. Repetition is a wonderful rhetorical strategy for emphasizing and giving clarity to a message.

"Any idea, plan, or purpose may be placed in the mind through repetition of thought."
Napoleon Hill, American Author

"Repetition of the same thought or physical action develops into a habit which, repeated frequently enough, becomes an automatic reflex."

Norman Vincent Peale,
Protestant Preacher and Author

3. Be Creative

Use various methods for communicating. Great communicators know that people learn and receive information in different ways, therefore, they employ creative ways to get the message across.

My wife, Joy, is an elementary school teacher and is one of the most brilliant and creative communicators I know. Countless times she has offered me tips before a public speaking opportunity that allowed me to engage with the audience better. She often challenges me by the various methods she uses to teach including music, games, humor, movies, and object lessons, along with other more traditional methods. Her students love it. It is no wonder to me why she is sought after by peers to teach workshops and conferences.

Before your next presentation, be sure to ask, "How can I make this more memorable?"

"The soul never thinks without a picture."

Aristotle, Greek Philosopher

4. Listen

Much of this section has dealt with methods for delivering information, but turn your focus on an aspect of communication that is often overlooked, listening. I have yet to teach a conference on communication where someone did not say that the attribute they value the most in a communicator is his/her ability to listen. It may be the greatest tool leaders have in order to gain respect by those he/she leads. I believe it was John Maxwell who said, "People don't care how much you know until they know how much you care."

"The ear of the leader must ring with the voices of the people."

Woodrow Wilson,
28th President of the United States

"Communication can't always follow the top-down model. With the fluidity of information in business today, leaders need to be masterful listeners; they need to be able to receive as well as send."

Joe Badaracco, Harvard Business School

"I need to hear from people about what they think…it is in the exchange of actually listening to others and my openness to act when appropriate that I am able to gain an ear of others in order to influence them."

Mohan Zachariah, Pastor

Excellent communication skills are so rare that when people possess such an ability, they are quick to assume leadership positions.

When I was in college, my pastor, Phil Wilson, gave me some advice about communicating. He said that if I will check myself in these 2 areas then I would avoid much unnecessary relational conflict. They are as follows:

2 Issues in Communication that will "Kill" Your Influence with Others

1. **Tone**

   Am I communicating with the right tone of voice? If not, do I need to take a minute to recompose myself before continuing? Am I sending my message in such a way that people feel threatened by my tone?

2. **Timing**

   Does this seem like a good time to bring this up to my recipient? Am I interrupting something more significant?

   A quick word about timing. Many have used this very thought as an excuse not to deal with behaviors or situations that need confronting. Some will reason to themselves, "this is not a good time," up to the point that they will never take action. My intent is simply for you to consider the recipient's circumstances before you communicate.

NOTES:

CHAPTER 4

RHYTHM: *Systems*

"Treat a man as he is, he will remain so. Treat a
man the way he can be and ought to be, and he will
become as he can be and should be."
Johann Wolfgang von Goethe, German Writer

"If we did the things we are capable of,
we would astound ourselves."
Thomas Edison, American Inventor

Continuing with the music analogy, rhythm is a strong, regular, repeated pattern of sound or movement. Without good rhythm, songs tend to drag or sound inconsistent. In some cases, they fall apart. As an example, consider the effect a drummer would have on the entire band if he couldn't keep a steady beat; it would not be pretty. I have been in live rehearsals where the rhythm sections were not on the same page and songs we were intending on performing were cut from the playlist. Yet, good music has a steady rhythm; it is often what separates the amateur musicians from professionals.

The same could be said about organizations. Healthy organizations have consistent patterns and systems in place that aid workflow and operations. Without these systems, companies experience high turnover among staff and customers. People are frustrated because there is little organization; they need systems that work.

Most of us know how frustrating it can be to work at a job where there are no systems in place. Whether it is uncertainty in filing insurance, approving an expense, ordering products, accepting returns, or not having a written job description, this can culminate for an unpleasurable organizational culture.

Key Point: Systems are highly important to organizations because they eliminate subjectivity.

5 Systems that Aid Organizational Consistency

1. Expectations
2. Performance
3. Recognition
4. Hiring/Termination
5. Professional Development

Let's take a moment to discuss the 5 systems.

Expectations
People need to know what is expected of them in their jobs. This is vital if we want to move them from looking at their work as a job to viewing it as their career. Within the organizations I consult, we develop people to become experts in their areas of proficiency. This cannot happen if they are being pulled in too many areas.

Employees cannot perform to our expectations if they are not aware of our expectations. I am always astounded at how many businesses operate without job descriptions and other tools that communicate the company's expectations of employees.

The following may be used to reinforce expectations:

- Job Descriptions
- Company Policies and Procedures
- Repetitive Communication
- Reasonable Deadlines

Performance

Systems should also be in place to manage performance. One of the worst places to be within an organization is the area of uncertainty concerning your job performance. In order to grow, people must be evaluated. Lencioni stated, performance systems serve to "help employees identify their opportunities for growth and development, and to constantly realign their work and their behaviors around the direction and values of the organization at large." The problem with the majority of performance systems is that they are way too complicated and tedious. It is necessary to make sure your system contains only pertinent information that encourages discussion around personal growth and development.

When I travel to facilitate, consult, or teach, I always distribute evaluation forms to the audience, especially those who hired me. The reason is because I would like to take every opportunity as a tool for growth both personally and professionally. I love to hear honest and objective feedback concerning my job performance. I believe as leaders we must be willing to be evaluated if we place this expectation upon others.

Consider implementing the following:

- Evaluations (individual performance measuring tool)
- Staff Meetings (collective performance measuring tool)
- Customer Service Surveys
- Competition Comparisons

Recognition

Organizations that are truly remarkable develop consistent criteria for recognizing employees. Regardless if the recognition includes bonuses, promotions, and other compensations, there should be no subjectivity in this area. Employees ought to have a clear road map of the behaviors and performances that earn recognition. In return, they are rewarded for behaving and performing in a manner that contributes to the company's success. Everybody wins when this happens.

Be creative when recognizing employees. In fact, let your team help you find creative ways to do so.

Systems of recognition may include:

- "Wowing" a Customer
- Goal Attainment
- Achieving Certification
- Personal Growth
- Embodiment of Company Values
- Fitness

Hiring/Termination

The healthiest organizations use objective criteria for hiring and termination.

Hiring: In the hiring process, questions should be asked that diagnose whether the potential hire possesses values that would make him/her a good fit within the company. Although resume items and skills can be helpful, they cannot be indicative of one's future success. As Henry Ford stated, "We hire a man, not his history." I always encourage organizations to hire based upon two criteria (beyond basic job competencies):

1. **Teachability**
   If a person is teachable, I am almost certain I can teach him/her how to be successful within an organization. If he/she is not teachable, there is almost nothing I can do to help this person succeed.

2. **Attitude**
   People who possess a consistently positive attitude are a huge asset to an organization. I love what Judith Knowlton said, "I discovered I always have choices and sometimes it's only a choice of attitude." A poor attitude is very difficult to correct.

If a person is teachable and has a consistently positive attitude, I can be fairly certain he will be a good fit. As well, hiring should be done in groups, leaving little room for decisions to be made that are subjective to one person's point of view.

Termination: Termination is typically a difficult area for most leaders. I know plenty of business executives who have flown in consultants to terminate an unruly employee. As Jeff Bezos of Amazon.com stated, "One of the key elements of being a good business leader is the capacity to tell the hard truths." No truth seems as hard as telling someone they are dismissed from their job. Therefore, leaders must allow the organization's values to discern their decisions in terminating an employee. Plus, they must have a system in place that helps guide them through the process.

I learned how difficult this can be at the young age of 22 when I had to dismiss a volunteer. When I was in graduate school, I was hired by a church as the worship leader and associate pastor. When I first came on staff, I immediately implemented some systems and procedures that I would follow when interviewing musicians and singers. It was a way that I could protect our congregation from people abusing the privileges that come along with being a leader and to make sure the team members possessed the values that were fundamental to the church's purpose. The way I saw it was that there should be standards that we should meet if we want to be leaders in the church. It just so happened that a lady who had been in the church for years and was accustomed to singing solos did not like my procedures. In fact, she didn't think she should have to follow them and expressed this verbally to her son, a deacon. As you can imagine, he expressed his concern to me. As best I could, I explained to him that the systems I was implementing were for the good of the whole church and that I was not holding his mother to a higher standard than anybody else. To my benefit, he supported my decision. Yet, I still had to explain to her that if she would not follow the procedures, she would be dismissed from the team. As a result, she was dismissed. By no means was it based upon *my* like or dislike of the woman, rather her inflexibility to be held to our team's values.

Do you feel like this was handled appropriately? What would you have done?

Professional Development

As mentioned earlier, if organizations are to grow, her people must grow. I am a huge proponent of allocating resources, time, and energy to developing people, myself included. People are either an organization's greatest asset or greatest liability. I choose to make them an asset. Therefore, systems should be in place to make sure that people are receiving training in these areas, such as:

- Continuing Education Courses
- Conferences
- Certifications
- On-site Training Workshops
- Off-site Training Workshops

• Degree Seeking Courses

The consulting company I work with, LA Consultants, Inc., has developed a criteria for professional development that I am quite pleased with; we call it the "Career Path." I am pleased to implement this within as many organizations as I am able. In short, employees have a clear road map of how to succeed. We have designed a path that, if followed, will allow employees to achieve certification in their field, increase their salary, help develop a business model for their company, and more.

We must never stop learning! As leaders, we must rise to the challenge by leading others to advance themselves both professionally and personally. We will never regret equipping our people to be the best they can be.

Questions for Reflection

1. What systems are in place that reinforce your expectations for staff?

2. If you were to ask your employees, would they view their work more as a job or as their career? What steps can you take to help them view their work as a career?

3. Do you perform consistent evaluations upon staff, clearly communicating their opportunities for growth and development?

4. What are your company's core values? Are you modeling the type of behavioral values that you wish for your staff to possess?

5. Do employees have a clear road map of behaviors and performances that earn recognition? If not, take a moment to gather an action plan.

6. What criteria are you using for hiring/termination?

7. What resources are you investing in your people for professional and personal development?

NOTES:

CHAPTER 5

AUDIENCE: *Service*

"The single most important thing to remember
about any enterprise is that there are no results
inside its walls. The result of a business
is a satisfied customer."
Peter Drucker, Writer & Management Consultant

"Do what you do so well that they will want to see
it again and bring their friends."
Walt Disney

When I think about bands that have an extensive audience base, I can't help but think of U2. It is no wonder to me why U2 concerts sell out so quickly. The band from Dublin, Ireland has experienced success on an international level, rivaled only by a few. Over and over again, they have found ways to broaden their audience base and have people continuously coming back for more. Why? They are simply the best at what they do and they somehow find a way to create great music. It shouldn't be ignored either that they have run a successful business through music, media, merchandise, and other mediums.

In this regard, I am their audience. If you were to scroll through my iTunes folder, you would find dozens of songs by the band as well as a book or two on my bookshelf. I have become a satisfied customer.

Now, let's talk business. How do we keep people coming back to our services for more? And, how can we separate ourselves from our peers? I believe the answer has to do with customer service.

According to a recent Internet search, Wikipedia defines customer service: "Customer service is a series of activities designed to enhance the level of customer satisfaction—that is, the feeling that product or service has met the customer expectation."

When I think of great customer service, a few names immediately come to mind: Walt Disney, Ritz-Carlton, Lexus, Chick-fil-A, Apple, Starbucks, Wachovia, and Southwest Airlines. You may have others that come to mind depending on your demographics, but I hope you would agree on these.

Each of these companies in their own respective way "roll out the red carpet" for their customers. It is this type of treatment that builds customer loyalty. I am fervent in my attempt to persuade businesses to adopt a passion for service.

Consider USAA, an insurance and financial service provider. In 2008, BusinessWeek ranked the company #1 as Customer Service Champs for the second time. Why? Keep in mind that in 2007, USAA put 12,400 "member service representatives" through 250,000 total hours of classes to reinforce basic training. Also, according to Forrester Research, Inc.'s annual customer advocacy survey, USAA received the highest rating among insurance companies for the fourth year in a row. One customer states, "My financial provider does what is best for me, not just its own bottom line." Again members say that USAA "simplifies their life rather than complicating things unnecessarily. How? One-call problem resolution, straightforward product explanations, and streamlined claims processing are all examples."

I love how USAA's CEO Joe Robles responded, "I believe USAA employees know our members and genuinely care about them more. We're here to build life-long relationships with our members and you don't do that without making their interest top priority."

Wow, does that sound like your business? Pretty remarkable, huh!?!

A few weeks ago I was consulting at an optometric practice just outside of Nashville, TN. An incident occurred the day before our departure and it would prove a timely lesson in customer service. A customer came in for her appointment with the optician to pick up her new Rx glasses and to ensure a proper fit. She recently bought a new pair of sunglasses from a local department store and believed to have brought them in with her to the appointment. After being fit for her Rx glasses, she proceeded to checkout and then to her vehicle. When she got to her car, she realized she did not have her sunglasses. She came back into the office and began looking; the office staff joined the search. To the customer's delight, she found her glasses, or so she thought. What she found was a brand new pair of the same brand, which had arrived to the office a day prior. She wasn't aware that they could not be her's because they contained ophthalmic lenses and were a model that isn't carried except in specific opticals. The doctor attempted to explain the mix-up to the customer but she was not understanding. In fact, she was outraged and left feeling like the office was taking advantage of her.

What would you do in this instance?

_____ Prove to the customer that she is wrong.
_____ Accuse the customer of trying to steal and fire her as a patient.

_____ Apologize for any misunderstanding and give her the glasses.

Why?

What did we do? We pulled the team together to discuss how to handle the situation. As you would imagine, we each had different feelings. Yet, someone from our team suggested we should call her back and apologize for any misunderstanding and give her the sunglasses. This is what we did.

I am certain that the small monetary loss in goods that this practice took is considerably less "expensive" than an angry customer who feels like her eye doctor is taking advantage of her. Sometimes excellent customer service isn't to our *immediate* benefit but rather is a long-term investment in the well-being and loyalty of our customers.

Do you have a customer satisfaction survey? If no, consider tracking customer experience using a survey or evaluation. What feedback would you be interested in hearing from your customers? Jot it down.

-
-
-
-

I would like to offer you a few customer service tips.

Top 10 Tips on How to Turn Customers into Fans

1. Offer solutions for problems.
2. Politely troubleshoot with customer.

3. Have a positive attitude regardless of circumstance.
4. Take the blame.
5. Genuinely apologize for any inconvenience and mean it.
6. Put yourself in their shoes; empathize.
7. Don't take problems personally.
8. Do what you say you are going to do.
9. Go beyond what the customer expected.
10. Smile.

Questions for Reflection:

1. If you were the customer, how would you feel about your business? Consider the areas in which your competition exceeds you in customer service.

-

-

-

2. Walk through with a customer. What were you impressions? How could your service improve?

-

-

-

3. What types of conversations are your customer service people having? Are they indicative of an area that needs attention?

4. Have you paid much attention to the area of customer service within your company? Why or why not? Do you think it is an area worthy of your time and focus? What needs to be changed or improved?

-

-

-

NOTES:

CHAPTER 6

LEADERSHIP ACTION PLAN:
Refining Your Leadership

"I'd like to be remembered as one who kept my
priorities in the right order. We live in a changing
world, but we need to be reminded that the important things have not changed,
and the important things will not change
if we keep our priorities in proper order."
Truett Cathy, Founder of Chick-fil-A Restaurant

"Exert your talents, and distinguish yourself, and
don't think of retiring from the world, until the
world will be sorry that you retire."
Samuel Johnson, English Literary Figure

A few years ago, Joy and I bought our first house together;
we were thrilled. When we moved in it was winter and
the grass was dead. Yet as summer rolled around, the colors
began to change and I saw the potential for a beautiful yard.
We had the perfect setting for a yard, as it resembled the
fairways of Augusta National (at least in my mind). We did
not have a single tree in our yard and the Bermuda grass was

like walking on carpet. Until...I decided to fertilize it. Little did I know that I would have to mow sometimes three times a week to keep up with the growth. It required more effort on my part, but the results were great.

There are things we can do to "fertilize" our leadership abilities.

Implementing the Leadership Action Plan is key. Over the next three years, I want you to monitor and seek to improve key relationships in your life, constantly asking the question, "How do I become a better leader?" Each of us has the ability to develop into healthy leaders: mentally, physically, and spiritually. I am also challenging you to cultivate your relationship to self, followers, peers, superiors, family, and God.

The leadership development action plan is as follows. The steps are broken down into the *4A's: A—analyze, A—apprehend, A—action, and A—adjust*. These 4 steps should be developed in order to routinely examine and hold yourself accountable to becoming a better leader.

Step 1: *Analyze*

In order to grow as a leader; you must continually seek to improve on your strengths and delegate your weaknesses. In order to do so, self-observation and evaluation from others will be vital. Christopher Neck, Tedd Mitchell, Charles Manz, and Emmet Thompson state, "The cement that lays the foundation for our self-leadership includes information we possess about ourselves—in other words, our self-awareness." In this step, you must examine the factors that lead to or distract from being productive; this sets the stage for understanding what steps need to be focused upon for growth. Complete the following:

Activities Leading to Production	Activities Distracting from Production

Key Point: Great leaders learn to capitalize on their strengths and delegate their weaknesses.

Step 2: *Apprehend*

After self-observation and evaluation from others, one must seek to understand why we do what we do, when we do it. If we have noticed undesirable behaviors and patterns within our leadership, we need to understand what makes us perform in this manner. We can then develop an action plan. Use the following evaluation for others to help determine your strengths and weaknesses.

Personal Evaluation

1. I am mostly viewed by others as being:

2. What talents and abilities do I possess that stand out above others?

3. I tend to dislike situations that cause me to:

4. What areas have I received affirmation regarding my giftedness?

5. What type of environments do I thrive in?

6. What type of environments do I avoid?

7. I consider the following to be a personal weakness:

8. What areas would benefit if I chose to delegate the tasks?

9. In what areas should I spend more time, capitalizing on my strengths?

Step 3: *Action*

Set attainable goals are important on the road to improvement. Small steps must be taken at first in order to accomplish great goals. One must realize that undesirable habits must be replaced with positive habits. Avoid general and unclear goals, rather be specific and set goals that are easily perceived; customize your plan according to your need.

Allow those closest to you to help you set realistic goals. In addition, it is important to set both short-term and long-term goals. Achieved short-term goals will add motivation for future goals; reward yourself when objectives are reached. It is worth noting that once steps 1 and 2 have been taken, starting your action plan must not be delayed.

Personal Action Plan

My undesirable behaviors/weaknesses are:

1.

2.

3.

My short-term goals in ridding/delegating these behaviors are:

My long term-goals in ridding/delegating these behaviors are:

The following people/systems are holding me accountable to these goals:

My positive behaviors/strengths are:

1.

2.

3.

My short-term goals in ridding/delegating these behaviors are:

My long term-goals in ridding/delegating these behaviors are:

The following people/systems are holding me accountable to these goals:

Step 4: *Adjust*
As most would attest, after an extended period of time, your development plan must be assessed and adjusted. Sometimes, we set unrealistic goals and need to set more attainable ones. Making these adjustments will help your plan last.

Strengthening the Whole Leader

A healthy leader ought to have a well-balanced approach to fitness. Three aspects of a leader's fitness will be considered: mental, physical, and spiritual. They will be dealt with in this order.

Mental: Mental fitness is equally as important to a leader's health as the other two components. Leaders are constantly pressed for time due to packed schedules, meetings, and deadlines. If they do not take time to be invested in themselves, they can quickly burn out. Due to the high level of responsibility leaders possess, it can be common for emotional exhaustion to set in, leading to a lack of production at work and raising conflict within the home.

I have noticed times in my life when I have become mentally exhausted. I recall a time when a sense of depression and stresses overwhelmed me. Many factors led to this state. For example, when I was in graduate school I took five courses and worked three part-time jobs. My routine was to leave at 6:30 am and not return home until between 9-11:00 pm. This occurred seven days a week for many months. It was an extremely stressful situation and I paid the consequences.

Since that time, I have taken steps to correct this type of behavior. Allowing myself a day of rest once a week and taking time for leisure activities have improved my mental fitness. Yet, there are some things I am incorporating in my life. Consider these ideas to implement in your life to aid your mental fitness:

1. **Continual Learning:** It is highly important that we continually develop mentally. One way to do so is to invest time and resources into personal education. Let me offer a few short-term and long-term goals you may adopt for yourself.

    a. *Short-term:* Read two books a month in an effort to keep your mind sharp and subscribe to a monthly magazine of personal interest.
    b. *Long-term:* Attend at least one conference a year that furthers your career skills.

2. **Leisure Activities:** Without leisure activities that allow time for reflection and rest, we often find ourselves with an unhealthy balance between "working to live" and "living to work."

    a. Short-term: Begin with a block of four hours every week where you can choose to be undistracted an uninterrupted from common responsibilities. This time can be spent in a number of activities such as hiking, swimming, golf, massage, biking, photography, etc.

    b. Long-term: Twice a year coordinate a two/three day trip with good friends and momentarily escape the responsibilities of work and home. Although this may seem unreasonable, everyone will benefit from your new perspective.

Physical: Physical activity sounds grueling to some, but is an important aspect to leadership fitness. Exercising has been proven to lower stress and makes one's life more productive. Energy levels are increased and endorphins are released in many activities that stimulate one's behavior. In addition to exercise, proper nutrition plays a tremendous role in being a capable leader.

A few years ago I noticed a significant decline in my ability to perform physically. For most of my life I was involved in athletics and competed at a collegiate level for four years. On average I ran approximately four miles a day. All of this to say that in graduate school, I attempted to approach nutrition in the same ways I had in college. Yet sitting in a classroom and working jobs that required little physical activity began to take a toll on my body. Not only did I gain weight, but also my energy decreased and I began to feel bad. My eating habits gradually became worse and I made excuses for my behavior. What I needed to do was take an honest look at my life and make changes in exercise and nutritional habits. Let's quickly look at both.

1. **Exercise:** As mentioned above, the benefits of exercise are numerous.

    a. Short-term: Over the next six months, plan to do cardiovascular exercise at least three days out of the week. This can include a 30-minute walk or jog, swimming, playing sports, or other similar activities.

    b. Short-term: Over the next six months, do resistance training at least twice a week. This includes push-ups, weight training, and similar activities.

    c. Long-term: Over the course of the next year, have a goal to be closer to your target BMI (body mass index). Track your progress.

2. **Nutrition:** Healthy eating habits and nutritional supplementation are beneficial to the entire body and can lead to an increase in energy, a faster metabolism, and improved health.

    a. Short-term: Over the next six months, cut back on fried foods, caffeine after 3:00 pm, and try to abstain from eating past 8:00 pm.

    b. Short-term: Consider eating desserts only on the weekend.

    c. Long-term: Begin a daily nutritional supplement and commit to it for a least a year. If you are uncertain about what to take, consider asking your doctor. Of course, I am partial to the nutritional company I represent and I proudly suggest Total Focus Vitamins (*www.totalfocusvitamins.com*).

Spiritual: It is easy to dishonor our commitments to spiritual growth, especially given the pace at which our lives are lived. Yet, I am of the firm belief that incorporating disciplines that help us grow in this area are imperative and too often overlooked or underemphasized. I want to help you become the best leader possible and that includes cultivating your soul.

Spiritual growth has been an extremely important aspect of my life for years. In fact, I have served in full-time leadership roles within churches for the bulk of my career. I still enjoy the pleasure of serving on staff at my local congregation.

Growing spiritually is fueled by spending time with God and cooperating fellowship with other believers. I am a Christian and find my highest purpose in life as a follower of Jesus. I cannot separate this from other aspects of my life; it is who I am. So for me, there are things I incorporate into my life to help me grow spiritually; as a result, my leadership ability and influence increase as well. Consider the following:

1. **Bible Study:** The Bible is complete with illustrations and lessons that are foundational to how we should live and serve one another. It specifically can lead you to become a remarkable person.

    a. *Short-term:* Begin with the book of John and read a section a day (sometimes this is just a few verses, sometimes more). After reading take a moment to journal afterward.

    b. *Long-term:* Attend a Bible Study for a semester. Churches have studies throughout the week and it should be easy to get plugged into.

2. **Prayer/Meditation:** Prayer is simply conversation with God, expressing to God what is on your heart and allowing time for Him to speak to you.

"Trust in the Lord with all your heart and do not lean on your own understanding. In all your ways acknowledge Him, and He will make your paths straight."

Proverbs 3:5-6

"Prayer is as natural expression of faith as breathing is of life."

Jonathan Edwards, Preacher and Theologian

Consider this prayer aid:

A: Adoration

Begin your prayers by expressing your adoration toward God.

"Every good thing given and every perfect gift is from above..."

James 1:17

C: Confession

Confess to God areas in which you fall short to His standards.

"...for all have sinned a fall short of the glory of God."

Romans 3:23

T: Thanksgiving

Consider all the ways that you have been blessed and express it in thanks toward God.

"Blessed be the God and Father of our Lord Jesus Christ, who has blessed us with every spiritual blessing in the heavenly places in Christ."

Ephesians 1:3

S: Supplication
Spend time praying for your needs as well as others' needs.

"And my God will supply all your needs according to His riches in glory in Christ Jesus."
Philippians 4:19

Cultivating Key Relationships

Becoming "fit to lead" requires improving existing relationships. Each of us neglects relationships that constantly need nourishing. In an effort to improve our most important relationships, I will examine them briefly. Six relationships will be looked at: self-to-self, self-to-followers, self-to-peers, self-to-superiors, self-to-family, and self-to-God.

Self-to-Self: One cannot effectively lead others until he leads himself. This is an important link that many leaders fail to connect. Self-leadership is one of the most difficult relationships for us to nurture because we often think of it as being selfish with our time. Yet, taking steps to improve one's mental, physical, and spiritual realms will greatly behoove a leader in his leadership to others.

Leadership expert Tim Elmore (*www.growingleaders. com*) states that lack of self-leadership is "common hazard" for leaders. He compares leaders who do not take time to lead themselves to "starving bakers." Elmore states, "It's the baker who spends so much time baking bread for others, he forgets to eat and starves himself." In order to be of help to others, we must first lead ourselves.

Self-to-Followers: If people don't follow you, then you aren't a leader. The relationship that you have with followers is important to continually nourish and keep healthy. Consider improving your communication with followers. As well, if you hold them to high expectations, make sure that you have clearly spelled them out. Communicate to them that adhering to agreed upon standards are priority and that they possess the power to keep you accountable to high standards as well. Be approachable, and express an invitation for followers to voice any concerns directly to you.

Self-to-Peers: Peers can often be the people you spend the most time with, especially in a work environment. These relationships need careful guidelines in order to be healthy due to the amount of time spent together. Improve these relationships by seeking professional advice from them. I have concluded that we can learn many valuable lessons from others' experiences, while also learning how to do our jobs more efficiently. As a project, plan to have lunch with one peer each week that works within the same field of practice.

Self-to-Superiors: Similar to your relationships with peers, stronger relationships with your superiors are very beneficial. Take advantage of the leaders you serve under. Make it a goal to meet regularly with your immediate superior in an environment in which you talk about work as well as life skills. If possible, plan to schedule lunch meetings with your immediate superior once a week and seek to do the same with community leaders once a month.

Self-to-Family: This is one of the most vital relationships that we have. I believe that my relationship with my family directly affects all others. My wife and I committed at marriage to keep a date night at least once a week. During this time, we turn off our cell phones and we focus our attention on our time together. Further, commit to be home from work at a reasonable time and don't break it unless your family is aware of the special circumstance. This helps your family feel important and allows you the boundary between personal and professional.

Self-to-God: I believe one's relationship with God is of greatest importance. Invest in this relationship and all others will be given the right priority.

I must tell you that my relationship with God has made all the difference in the world for me. I honestly believe that every person would live a vastly more satisfying life if God's love, grace, and redemption were operating in their lives. I'll do my best to explain.

We learn who God is through the Bible. It teaches that God has revealed Himself to us through the person of Jesus, God's own Son. In fact, the Bible teaches us that we are all born with the desire to turn away from God; we are sinners. What this means is that we don't naturally love God, rather we do things such as lie for our benefit, cheat to get ahead, and steal to gain. We don't always do these things in public and would rarely admit these behaviors, but we have all done them. But it is deeper than just our actions; our hearts are deceitful.

Because of our sin, we cannot have proper relationship with God; it separates us from Him. It is for this reason that God would provide a way to restore our relationship to Him. God knows what is in the heart of man and prepared from the beginning to send His Son, Jesus, to die as a substitute for our sin.

The Bible says, "For God so loved the world, that He gave His only unique Son, that whoever believes in Him would not perish, but have eternal life" (John 3:16).

God sent Jesus to live a perfect life and die an unfair death. The Bible says, "God demonstrates His own love toward us, in that while we were still sinners, Christ died for us" (Romans 5:8). This begs the question: "Why would God go to such lengths to prove His love?" But Jesus said, "I came to seek and to save what was lost." Jesus reveals to us that God loves people and would even give His Son in order to restore our relationship to Him.

I know this sounds quite religious, but it is much more than that. I personally am not a big proponent of religious activity unless it is for the benefit of all people. Rather, this is God's invitation to you and I to accept the gift of grace that He offers when we place our faith in Him.

If you have any questions, I would love for you to visit a website that explains this in much better detail than I am able: www.twowaystolive.com.

CONCLUSION

It is my sincere hope that *A Remarkable Practice* has been a practical, strong tool to help you better understand the dynamics of your organization as well as further develop your leadership ability. The characteristics that make an organization great are common regardless of the industry you are in. People who have the privilege to work in these environments are blessed.

For those who do not work in such an environment, it is likely that you are experiencing high turnover and low production. I am confident you now have some tools to help turn things around. Take to heart the content of this book and use it to diagnose the areas that need attention.

And for you who have the awesome privilege to be leaders, I encourage you to grow in your abilities and further develop a heart for the people. For it is people we lead and we are only worth following if we genuinely care for others.

It would be for my benefit to receive your feedback concerning *A Remarkable Practice*. I ask that you feel free to visit www.aremarkablepractice.com and leave me a note with your encouragement and suggestions.

And, it would be my pleasure to serve you by scheduling an onsite consult or a leadership development workshop. Email: info@aremarkablepractice.com.

Thank you!

Privileged to Lead,

Ben Finch

Printed in the United States
131395LV00002B/1-300/P